DEALING WITH ADDICTION
DRUG AND ALCOHOL ADDICTION

by Sheila Llanas

BrightPoint Press

San Diego, CA

© 2023 BrightPoint Press
an imprint of ReferencePoint Press, Inc.
Printed in the United States

For more information, contact:
BrightPoint Press
PO Box 27779
San Diego, CA 92198
www.BrightPointPress.com

ALL RIGHTS RESERVED.

No part of this work covered by the copyright hereon may be reproduced or used in any form or by any means—graphic, electronic, or mechanical, including photocopying, recording, taping, web distribution, or information storage retrieval systems—without the written permission of the publisher.

Content Consultant: Ken Winters, PhD, Senior Scientist at the Oregon Research Institute (MN location), Adjunct Faculty in the Department of Psychology, University of Minnesota

---

LIBRARY OF CONGRESS CATALOGING-IN-PUBLICATION DATA

Names: Llanas, Sheila Griffin, 1958- author.
Title: Drug and alcohol addiction / by Sheila Llanas.
Description: San Diego, CA: BrightPoint Press, an imprint of ReferencePoint Press, Inc., [2023] | Series: Dealing with addiction | Includes bibliographical references and index. | Audience: Grades 10-12
Identifiers: LCCN 2022008671 (print) | LCCN 2022008672 (eBook) | ISBN 9781678203740 (hardcover) | ISBN 9781678203757 (eBook)
Subjects: LCSH: Drug addiction--Juvenile literature. | Alcoholism--Juvenile literature.
Classification: LCC RC564.3 .L525 2023 (print) | LCC RC564.3 (eBook) | DDC 362.29--dc23/eng/20220316
LC record available at https://lccn.loc.gov/2022008671
LC eBook record available at https://lccn.loc.gov/2022008672

CONTENTS

AT A GLANCE	4
INTRODUCTION	6
LOSING CONTROL	
CHAPTER ONE	12
WHAT IS DRUG AND ALCOHOL ADDICTION?	
CHAPTER TWO	26
THE SCIENCE OF DRUG AND ALCOHOL ADDICTION	
CHAPTER THREE	36
THE EFFECTS OF DRUG AND ALCOHOL ADDICTION	
CHAPTER FOUR	48
TREATING DRUG AND ALCOHOL ADDICTION	
Glossary	58
Source Notes	59
For Further Research	60
Index	62
Image Credits	63
About the Author	64

AT A GLANCE

- Drug and alcohol addiction is a chronic illness of the brain.

- Substance use damages the brain's normal growth.

- There is no cure for addiction. Treatment helps patients get sober.

- Drugs and alcohol can be habit-forming. Addiction is when a person continues to use a drug even when it is harmful.

- More than 39 million Americans aged twelve and older use illicit drugs. Close to 140 million drink alcohol. About 19.3 million Americans aged eighteen and older have an addiction problem.

- In 2021, there were more than 100,000 overdose deaths in the United States.

- Addiction targets every age, race, and gender. Trauma, neglect, or abuse can raise the likelihood of addiction.

- Teenagers are at a high risk for drug addiction. Early use is more likely to lead to addiction.

- Programs such as Alcoholics Anonymous and Narcotics Anonymous support people in recovery.

INTRODUCTION

LOSING CONTROL

In ninth grade, Jamey changed schools. He felt shy and insecure. A classmate offered him marijuana. "Take a hit," David said. "Weed won't hurt you. Everyone does it."

Jamey felt instant relief. His stress melted. He no longer felt anxious.

Jamey wanted more of these feelings. He smoked daily, before and after school. He got high at night. Some days, he cut back. But it was hard to fight the cravings.

Friends and classmates may pressure someone into trying drugs.

Before his senior year, Jamey tried to quit. An odd thing happened. He had no emotions. He felt numb and empty. His grades slipped. He spent less time with his friends. He spent whole days sitting on the couch. His mother knew that Jamey was not well. She took him to the doctor. The doctor said that Jamey was addicted to marijuana. Jamey had used the drug heavily for three years. But he never thought he was addicted.

Jamey got **sober**. He joined a support group for teens in recovery. He learned who he was without marijuana. He no

Support groups can help people recover from drug or alcohol addiction.

longer felt numb. He learned to clearly express his emotions. He liked being in the group. Everyone was there to deal with similar issues.

THAT FIRST TIME

Addiction starts with a first time. It may be a first time smoking. It could be a first sip of beer. "A friend offers you something at a party or at home," says Dr. Deeni Bassam, a pain specialist. "Or you're having a bad day and you need something to pick you up. . . . That's how this problem always starts."[1]

Jamey's classmate David said marijuana was safe to use. He was wrong. Any substance is unsafe if overused. Teenagers are at high risk of becoming addicted to alcohol and other drugs. Teens become

Teens are especially at risk of developing a drug or alcohol addiction.

addicted more often than adults do. In 2019, 4.8 million Americans aged 12 and over had a marijuana use disorder. Addiction can be deadly. The illness is hard to treat. Jamey was lucky. He got help.

1. WHAT IS DRUG AND ALCOHOL ADDICTION?

Drug and alcohol addiction is a brain disorder. When people are addicted, substance use is not a choice. They need drugs to feel well or normal. An addicted person uses the drug even if it hurts them. Drug use becomes the priority in their lives.

Addiction is a serious problem in the United States. In 2019, 14.5 million Americans aged twelve and older had an alcohol use disorder. In 2021, more than 100,000 Americans died of drug overdoses.

Addiction causes people to abuse alcohol or other drugs despite the pain it causes.

One out of four people who tries heroin gets addicted to it. Every day, close to 130 Americans die of an opioid overdose. Marijuana is also addictive.

DEFINING ADDICTION AS A DISEASE

In the 1800s, drinking alcohol was common. People drank together for business and fun. Young single men tended to drink the most.

At the time, doctors knew little about addiction. They saw healthy people die from drinking too much. Doctors realized something. Drinking too much was not simply a bad choice. It was a sickness.

Alcohol addiction has affected people throughout history.

The doctors' observations helped define drug and alcohol addiction as a disease.

Much of society still considered addiction a result of bad choices. People who became addicted were judged. They were seen as weak and as failures. New drugs came on the market. In the 1920s, drugstores sold morphine and cocaine as pain relievers. Few people knew these drugs were habit-forming. "Doctors and patients alike were tempted to overuse,"

THE PROHIBITION ACT

In 1920, the United States wanted to end alcoholism. Congress passed the Prohibition Act. It banned making and selling alcohol. The ban did not work as intended. People brewed homemade liquor. They sold it at illegal bars. Drinking did not end. It simply became illegal. Prohibition ended in 1933.

wrote David T. Courtwright.[2] His book *Dark Paradise* studied addiction in America.

It took a long time for doctors to call addiction an illness. Starting in 1952, the diagnostic manual of the American Psychiatric Association (APA) considered addiction a major mental illness. The American Medical Association (AMA) defined alcoholism as a medical illness in 1956. Alcoholism is the disease of being addicted to alcohol. In 1987, the AMA defined all addiction as a medical illness. The definition is important. Calling addiction a medical disease has led to better health

OxyContin is the brand name of oxycodone, a highly addictive painkiller.

care and treatment. Today, doctors use another term for addiction. They call the disease substance use disorder (SUD).

WHAT DRUGS ARE ADDICTIVE?

Many substances can be addictive. Some are legal. Others are not. In much of the United States, adults can legally buy alcohol, tobacco, and marijuana. Oxycodone is legal as a prescription drug. All of those substances are highly addictive. Being legal does not make a drug safe.

Alcohol is made from grains, fruits, yeasts, and sugars. It is a **depressant**. Alcohol dulls the nervous system. It causes mood swings. Males aged eighteen to twenty-five are at the highest risk of abusing alcohol. Men in that age-group tend to

Marijuana has been bred to be much stronger than in previous decades.

binge drink. Repeated drinking can lead to addiction.

Marijuana comes from cannabis plants. The flowers are dried. The drug is rolled into cigarettes and smoked. It is also made into concentrated oils. Hash is a strong form of marijuana. The mind-altering agent in marijuana is tetrahydrocannabinol (THC).

Cocaine comes from coca leaves. The white powder is snorted through the nose. It goes into the bloodstream to reach the brain. Crack cocaine is cocaine that has been boiled and dried into rocks. There is no safe level of cocaine or crack. Even one use can lead to addiction.

Meth is short for methamphetamine. Meth is a bitter, white powder. It is very toxic. It is made illegally from

Crystal meth excites the nervous system and can cause paranoia.

store-bought chemicals. Crystal meth comes in rock form.

Cocaine and meth are **stimulants**. They excite the nervous system. They provide energy, alertness, and a sense of being powerful. They can also make people angry or violent.

Opioids block pain. They make users calm, happy, and sleepy. Opioids can cause nausea and slow breathing. Some opioids are made in a lab. Others come from the poppy plant. Doctors prescribe the opioids morphine and codeine as painkillers. Illegal opioids, such as heroin, are more dangerous.

WHO GETS ADDICTED?

No one plans to become addicted to alcohol and other drugs. No single thing causes addiction. Addiction may be linked to someone's genetics and environment. It could be linked to family dynamics and personality. Living in an unsafe neighborhood is a risk factor. So is easy access to drugs. Bullying and parental neglect may make someone more likely

SUBSTANCE ABUSE VERSUS ADDICTION

Substance abuse does not always lead to addiction. Abuse is using a drug the wrong way. Taking too much is abuse. Binge drinking is abuse. Some people who abuse drugs can stop. Other people who abuse a drug get addicted. They want to quit. Their disease makes them use the substance anyway.

to abuse substances. So might having an addicted family member. Suffering from a mental illness and exposure to trauma are also risk factors. However, none of these risk factors guarantee that someone will become addicted.

Addiction can happen to anyone. They could be young or old, male or female, rich or poor. It crosses borders of class, race, and education.

2
THE SCIENCE OF DRUG AND ALCOHOL ADDICTION

Alcohol and other drugs change how people act. A drunk person cannot walk straight. A person high on marijuana might stare into space. Someone on cocaine might drive in a dangerous way.

Parts of the brain rule actions and emotions. Alcohol and other drugs change those areas. Teens who abuse drugs often have short attention spans. They experience memory loss. They may have lower IQ levels. These losses can last even after drug use stops.

Drug or alcohol addiction affects a person's memory and ability to learn.

People may ignore warnings about the effects of drug use on brain development.

Nic Sheff became addicted to drugs as a teenager. "I'd heard all those warnings about pot affecting brain development and all that, but I thought it was a scare tactic."[3] He noticed changes to his emotions, memory, and ability to learn.

WHY ARE TEENS PRONE TO ADDICTION?

The brain does not fully form until early adulthood. It is still growing during the teenage years. Teens are learning to make choices. They may not think about the pros and cons of their decisions. They tend to seek excitement. They do not think about the downside of taking risks.

Sheff was able to get sober. He wrote about his addiction to help others avoid it. "Looking back, I realized I spent so much of high school and college high, that I missed a lot of what normally happens during those years. It's when I should have learned how to . . . deal with all the normal pressures of adolescent life."[4]

HOW DO DRUGS AND ALCOHOL CHANGE THE BRAIN?

Addiction is linked to dopamine, a brain chemical. Dopamine makes the body

DRUG AND ALCOHOL ADDICTION SLANG

Many words for being on drugs sound negative. Some are *wasted*, *buzzed*, and *fried*. Others are *stoned*, *bombed*, and *hammered*. These slang words show how drugs make people feel. They suggest how substances damage the brain.

Addiction causes people to miss out on important events and relationships.

feel good. It is a sign of pleasure. Exercise and laughter release healthy levels of dopamine. They make a person feel good.

Drugs also feel good, but they are not healthy. Drugs trick the brain. It releases too much dopamine. Dopamine levels do not go back to normal. The next use of the drug does not feel as good. The brain releases less dopamine. It takes a bigger dose to achieve the same reward in the brain.

Ryan was addicted to illegal drugs. At first, it felt good. Then his body got used to it. He needed more and more to get that feeling. "Drugs and alcohol to me are the opposite of fun," Ryan said in recovery. "I had gotten to a point in my life where it wasn't fun. It was a . . . chore."[5]

When someone stops taking drugs, the brain releases less dopamine. This causes **withdrawal**. Withdrawal is a shock

HOW THE BRAIN RESPONDS TO MARIJUANA

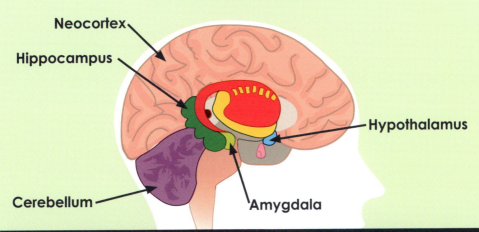

Brain Part	Controls	Response to Marijuana
Neocortex	high level thinking and feeling	poor thinking, loss of judgement, numb emotions
Hippocampus	learning new information, memory	loss of memory
Amygdala	emotions, regulates fear, evaluates threats	paranoia, anxiety, irrational fear
Cerebellum	movement and motor skills such as walking, reaching, and grabbing	slowed reflexes, loss of coordination, lack of balance
Hypothalamus	heart rate, hunger, and thirst	slowed heart rate, change in appetite, abnormal thirst

Source: "The Science of Marijuana: How THC Affects the Brain," Scholastic, 2011. http://headsup.scholastic.com.

Drugs and alcohol change how the brain functions. This chart describes normal brain function and the brain's response to marijuana.

to the body. It is common to feel body aches, chills, and fever. Someone may vomit, shake, sweat, or lose their appetite. The person may be moody, angry, or sad. Extreme symptoms may last days or weeks. Withdrawal is hard but important. It helps

NEW WORDS FOR DRUG ADDICTION

Medical experts have debated the word *addiction*. It causes people to think the illness is a single disorder. In reality, it is a problem with many factors. The word *addiction* separates the disorder from a person's other behavioral and mental disorders. This can lead to cultural **stigma**. It can also make it harder for someone to access health care. Doctors prefer to call drug and alcohol addiction a substance use disorder (SUD).

break the habit of using substances. With support, a patient can recover.

HOW ARE ADDICTIONS DIAGNOSED?

Addiction is hard to diagnose. Every case is unique. Doctors check a patient's habits and emotions. They screen for mental and social health.

Doctors use a standard test. They ask about health, habits, and quality of life. The purpose is to see if a problem exists or not. If addiction is present, the next step is to seek treatment.

3
THE EFFECTS OF DRUG AND ALCOHOL ADDICTION

Addicted people do things they would not do sober. They might put themselves in physical danger. They might be a danger to others.

"[Addiction] is much stronger than you. And it will win," says Trish. Her daughter died of an overdose. "This doesn't just affect you. It affects everybody in your family for the rest of their lives. . . . We're the ones stuck here, missing you. And there's help out there. You gotta take it."[6]

Driving while intoxicated can have disastrous results.

Addiction affects a person's relationships. Friends, teachers, and coworkers will worry, be hurt, and want to help. Addiction affects communities too. Schools, churches, medical clinics, and police departments deal with problems caused by addiction. Addiction affects everyone.

FIELD SOBRIETY TEST

Driving under the influence of alcohol or other drugs is illegal. Police officers use a three-part test to see if a driver is intoxicated. They check if the driver has clear vision. They test if the driver can walk in a straight line. They ask the driver to stand on one leg. Failing these tests can lead to arrest.

EFFECTS ON INDIVIDUAL BEHAVIOR

Addiction affects how the brain and body operate. It changes how a person behaves. The changes are not always for the better. On drugs, people may turn selfish, abusive, and controlling. They may lie, blame others, steal from loved ones, and commit crimes.

It is common for someone to hide their illness. They may want to spare loved ones. A person may deny she is sick. She may stop going to school or work. Someone may stop taking care of his body. He may forget to eat and sleep. He may become distant with loved ones.

Addiction causes people to do things they otherwise would not do, such as steal.

Some people struggle with severe addiction. They do not take care of themselves. They may be in poor health or in trouble. They could be broke, homeless, or hungry. People may want to keep their addiction a secret. But often, the signs of addiction give their secret away.

OVERDOSE

An overdose happens when alcohol or another drug overwhelms the body. The drug levels get too high. The drug becomes toxic in the body. This can be fatal.

Overdose risks are heart attack, seizure, and stroke. Other risks are organ failure and coma. On stimulants, the heart rate and breathing are too fast. An opioid overdose is the opposite. Breathing slows or stops.

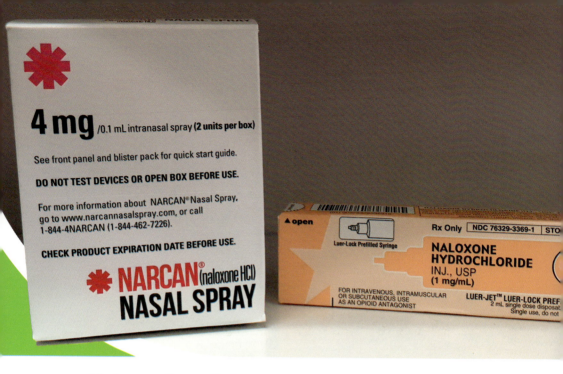

Naloxone is available through a pharmacist.

A drug called naloxone can reverse an opioid overdose. First responders and community members can carry the drug. Naloxone reverses the effects of opioids. The person snaps awake. Life-saving naloxone causes instant withdrawal. This can cause pain. Naloxone's effects are temporary. The overdose may continue after the drug's use. It is important for someone to receive medical care immediately after an overdose.

No drug can reverse an alcohol overdose. A person could choke, vomit, or black out. She should go to the hospital. Paramedics will give the patient oxygen and fluids. They might pump the patient's stomach to get rid of the alcohol.

EFFECTS ON COMMUNITIES

Addiction affects communities. Many agencies help people in addiction.

Police officers and the courts try to protect them. Paramedics and firefighters rush to save lives and treat injuries. Faith groups and social workers support people with addiction. These professionals often work together to help.

OPIOID EPIDEMIC

In the late 1990s, Purdue Pharma marketed a new painkiller to physicians. It was called OxyContin. Purdue urged doctors to prescribe OxyContin to patients. The company said the opioid was safe. They said it had a low risk of addiction. This was not true. OxyContin and other opioids are highly addictive. Between 1999 and 2019, nearly 500,000 people died of opioid overdoses in the United States.

Some cities offer safe places for people to use drugs. Staff provide clean tools. They offer health care, counseling, and drug treatment.

Solving addiction and related problems is difficult. Community members can feel overwhelmed. Negative public opinion does not help. "We call it a disease. We say that people with addiction should be helped, not blamed," wrote Brendan de Kenessey. He studies the **ethics** of how communities treat addiction. "But deep down, many of us still [think] that they could stop using if they tried harder."[7] This type of thinking makes

First responders are prepared to help people when they overdose.

it difficult to see addiction as a disease.

This can affect how a community responds to addiction.

PREVENTING DRUG AND ALCOHOL ADDICTION

Some prevention methods are working. The National Institute on Drug Abuse studied drug use in eighth, tenth, and twelfth graders. "In all three grades, we've seen a reduction in prescription-opioid misuse," said Dr. Wilson Compton.[8]

One prevention approach that works is reducing the supply of drugs. Stopping the sale of illegal drugs could keep people safer. If drugs were not available, fewer people would try them. Addiction might decline.

Another approach is reducing the interest in drugs. It takes strength to resist peer pressure. With help, teens may be less likely to try alcohol and other drugs.

4
TREATING DRUG AND ALCOHOL ADDICTION

Addiction to alcohol or other drugs is treatable. But only 11 percent of people experiencing addiction get treatment. Many people lack good health care. Other people do not want to quit using.

Medical treatment can help a person stop using drugs. But recovery is more than medical treatment. People also need help in other areas. They may need housing, jobs, and childcare. They may need mental health counseling.

People struggling with addiction do best when treated with respect. Abbie was on

Choosing to seek treatment is a big step for someone addicted to alcohol or other drugs.

the television show *16 and Recovering*. She said, "[The counselor] doesn't treat us like we're bad. She treats us like we're sick, because we are. Because addiction is a disease. It's not a choice."[9]

SEEKING TREATMENT

Recovering from addiction takes a series of steps. First, someone must decide to seek treatment. Some treatment programs are at inpatient facilities. This means people temporarily move into the **rehabilitation** center. Others are outpatient programs.

People are able to stay in their homes or other safe spaces during treatment.

People in treatment face the problems their addiction created. They deal with depression, regrets, and bad thoughts. They express emotions. They learn who they are without alcohol or other drugs.

SUPPORT GROUPS

Alcoholics Anonymous, or AA, helps with alcohol addiction. Narcotics Anonymous, or NA, is for people with drug addiction. These programs support long-term sobriety and recovery. They help people face their addictions. They guide people to recovery. Group members support each other. Sponsors are people who have been in recovery for some time. They guide new people to help them stay sober.

With counseling, patients begin to forgive themselves. Many feel grateful to be alive.

The risk of **relapse** is high at first. Withdrawal is severe. The pain can make people quit treatment. In some cases, doctors can replace a dangerous drug with a safer one. Methadone is a substitution treatment for heroin. It must be given under a doctor's care. Methadone cuts the craving for heroin. It helps patients quit. The desire to use drugs may never go away. The longer a person stays sober, the better their chances of recovery. Natural dopamine levels are restored.

Staying sober helps a person recover and enjoy other activities.

TYPES OF ADDICTION TREATMENT

There are several ways to treat addiction. Most rehabilitation centers use several different models. "A quality rehab program helps patients learn to manage the symptoms of the disease," explain the experts at Hazelden Betty Ford.[10]

Hazelden Betty Ford is a treatment provider. Most treatments involve changing a person's behavior.

Cognitive behavioral therapy (CBT) explores thought patterns. Thought patterns can lead to destructive behaviors, such as abusing drugs or alcohol. CBT helps people recognize these thought patterns. Then, it teaches patients how to change them. Dialectical behavioral therapy (DBT) focuses on behavioral change too. It also trains people how to calm down when upset.

Other treatment options use medications to treat addiction. Several drugs ease opioid withdrawal symptoms. Methadone is one example. Naltrexone is another. This drug is also used to treat alcohol addiction. It blocks the receptors in the brain that make alcohol and other drug use enjoyable.

HANDLING FAMILY DRUG PROBLEMS

Support groups help teenagers cope with a loved one's addiction. The Narateen group is part of Narcotics Anonymous. Alcoholics Anonymous Family Groups runs Alateen. The groups allow teenagers to talk with others about life with an addicted sibling, parent, or friend.

Mental health services are part of addiction treatment. People struggling with addiction often experience other conditions. These can include depression, anxiety, and trauma. Treating these issues during recovery can make treatment more successful.

Seeking and completing treatment are the first steps in recovery. Addiction is a chronic brain disease. It does not have a cure. This means people manage their symptoms for life. Many choose to take advantage of support groups. Others continue mental health treatment.

The first step toward healing addiction is seeking help.

Choosing treatment can be scary. Many people in recovery want to help those who are addicted. They know how hard it is. They also know that recovery is possible.

GLOSSARY

binge drink

to have four or more alcoholic drinks in two hours or less

depressant

a substance that slows a body's functions

ethics

a set of principles that a group abides by

rehabilitation

returning to an alcohol- or drug-free state

relapse

to have symptoms again after they improved

sober

not using alcohol or any other drug

stigma

negative, unfair beliefs that are widely shared

stimulants

substances that excite the nervous system

withdrawal

painful physical and psychological symptoms after stopping drug or alcohol use

SOURCE NOTES

INTRODUCTION: LOSING CONTROL

1. Quoted in "Chasing the Dragon," *FBI*, n.d. www.fbi.gov.

CHAPTER ONE: WHAT IS DRUG AND ALCOHOL ADDICTION?

2. Quoted in Erick Trickey, "America's 19th Century Opiate Addiction," *Smithsonian Magazine*, January 4, 2018. www.smithsonianmag.com.

CHAPTER TWO: THE SCIENCE OF DRUG AND ALCOHOL ADDICTION

3. David Sheff and Nic Sheff, *High*. Boston, MA: Houghton Mifflin Harcourt, 2019, p. 6.

4. Sheff and Sheff, *High*, p. 6.

5. Elaine McMillion Sheldon (Director), *Recovery Boys*, Netflix, 2018.

CHAPTER THREE: THE EFFECTS OF DRUG AND ALCOHOL ADDICTION

6. Quoted in "Chasing the Dragon," *FBI*, n.d. www.fbi.gov.

7. Brendan de Kenessey, "We Misunderstand How Those with Addiction Think," *The Big Idea* (blog), *Vox*, March 16, 2018. www.vox.com.

8. Quoted in Scott Simon, "Teen Drug Use Is Declining, but Why?" *National Public Radio*, March 18, 2017. www.npr.org.

CHAPTER FOUR: TREATING DRUG AND ALCOHOL ADDICTION

9. Quoted in "Where Are They Now? Abbie," *MTV*, September 23, 2020. www.youtube.com.

10. "The Hazelden Betty Ford Treatment Model: A Patient-Centered Path to Treating Alcohol and Drug Addiction," *Hazelden Betty Ford Foundation*, 2021. www.hazeldenbettyford.org.

FOR FURTHER RESEARCH

BOOKS

James J. Crist, *What's the Big Deal About Addictions? Answers and Help for Teens*. Minneapolis, MN: Free Spirit Publishing, 2021.

Susan E. Hamen, *Heroin and Its Dangers*. San Diego, CA: BrightPoint Press, 2020.

David Sheff and Nic Sheff, *High: Everything You Want to Know About Drugs, Alcohol, and Addiction*. Boston, MA: Houghton Mifflin Harcourt, 2019.

INTERNET SOURCES

American Addiction Centers Editorial Staff, "5 Controversial Thoughts We Have About Addiction," *American Addiction Centers*, June 11, 2019. https://drugabuse.com.

"Chasing the Dragon: The Life of an Opiate Addict," *FBI*, n.d. www.fbi.gov.

"Do You Have a Problem with Alcohol?" *Recovered*, 2021. https://ncadd.org.

WEBSITES

Drug Abuse Statistics
https://drugabusestatistics.org

Discover the numbers behind drug abuse at the National Center for Drug Abuse Statistics website.

NIDA
https://teens.drugabuse.gov/teens

NIDA is the National Institute on Drug Abuse. Learn drug facts, play games, and read the blog.

SAMHSA
www.samhsa.gov

SAMHSA is the Substance Abuse and Mental Health Services Administration. SAMHSA offers a National Helpline. If you or someone you love is in trouble with drugs or alcohol, or if they have a mental health issue, call or log on to talk to a counselor. Call 1-800-662-HELP (4357) or visit www.samhsa.gov/find-help/national-helpline for help.

INDEX

Alcoholics Anonymous, 51, 55
alcoholism, 16, 17
American Medical Association (AMA), 17
American Psychiatric Association (APA), 17

binge drinking, 19–20, 24

cocaine, 16, 21, 22, 26
codeine, 23
cognitive behavioral therapy (CBT), 54

depressants, 19
dialectical behavioral therapy (DBT), 54
dopamine, 30–32, 52

Hazelden Betty Ford, 54
heroin, 14, 23, 52

marijuana, 6, 8, 10, 11, 14, 19, 20–21, 26, 33
methadone, 52, 55
methamphetamine, 21–22
morphine, 16, 23

naloxone, 42
naltrexone, 55
Narcotics Anonymous, 51, 55
National Institute on Drug Abuse, 46

opioids, 14, 23, 41, 42, 44, 47, 55
overdoses, 13, 14, 36, 41–43, 44
oxycodone, 19
OxyContin, 44

prescription drugs, 19
Purdue Pharma, 44

recovery, 8, 32, 48, 51, 52, 56, 57
rehabilitation, 50, 53

Sheff, Nic, 28, 29
signs of alcohol or other drug addiction, 6–7, 26–27, 32, 39–40
stimulants, 22, 41
substance use disorder (SUD), 18, 34
symptoms of alcohol or other drug addiction, 8, 35, 41–43

tobacco, 19
treatment of alcohol or other drug addiction, 8–9, 50–52, 53–55, 56, 57

United States, 12, 16, 19, 44

withdrawal, 32–34, 42, 52, 55

IMAGE CREDITS

Cover: © Novikov Alex/Shutterstock Images
5: © Syda Productions/Shutterstock Images
7: © Photographee EU/Shutterstock Images
9: © VH Studio/Shutterstock Images
11: © Monkey Business Images/Shutterstock Images
13: © Fizkes/Shutterstock Images
15: © Everett Collection/Shutterstock Images
18: © Pure Radiance Photo/Shutterstock Images
20: © HQuality/Shutterstock Images
22: © Kaesler Media/Shutterstock Images
27: © Little NY Stock/Shutterstock Images
28: © Kryzhov/Shutterstock Images
31: © Srdjan Randjelovic/Shutterstock Images
33: © Gray Jay/Shutterstock Images
37: © Suzanne Tucker/Shutterstock Images
40: © Yakobchuk Viacheslav/Shutterstock Images
42: © Pure Radiance Photo/Shutterstock Images
46: © Delores M. Harvey/Shutterstock Images
49: © Motortion Films/Shutterstock Images
53: © Monkey Business Images/Shutterstock Images
57: © Raw Pixel/Shutterstock Images

ABOUT THE AUTHOR

Sheila Llanas writes informational books for young people. Her favorite topics include poetry, literature, art, nature, animals, culture, food, and health. She taught writing at the Johns Hopkins Center for Talented Youth and the University of Wisconsin–Waukesha.